Bernard Malamud
An Annotated Checklist

Bernard Malamud

An Annotated Checklist

By Rita Nathalie Kosofsky
University of Maryland

The Kent State University Press

The Serif Series
Bibliographies and Checklists, Number 7

William White, General Editor
Wayne State University

Standard Book Number 87338-037-1
Library of Congress Card Catalogue Number 75-626236
Manufactured in the United States of America
at the press of The Oberlin Printing Company
Designed by Merald E. Wrolstad

First Edition

Contents

Preface

In the sixteen years since the publication of his first book, *The Natural*, Bernard Malamud has achieved the stature of a major American author, having enjoyed popular and critical success, and having been awarded two National Book Awards and the Pulitzer Prize for Literature. In the chronicle of Malamud's private and literary lives, one can trace some of the steps he has taken in the development of his craft. One can see in the accumulation of reviews of his books and in the articles devoted to the criticism of his work the stimulating effect his writing has had upon the critical community; it has tantalized them to discern his artistic ancestors and challenged them to fit his work into a contemporary category. More important, Malamud's work has expressed significant themes and has demonstrated distinctive qualities to which readers and critics have been responsive.

The outward chronicle of the events of Malamud's life and literary career is consistent with the matter and manner of his work. He was born in Brooklyn in 1914, to Bertha Fidelman Malamud and Max Malamud. His parents were Jewish immigrants from Russia who eked out a meager living from a small grocery store in the Gravesend Avenue section of Brooklyn. Despite their poverty and lack of formal education, they encouraged young Malamud's desire for education and his ambition to become a writer. His experiences in Brooklyn,

his closeness to his parents and their memories, and his
observation of his neighbors' lives are reflected in his stories.

From 1928 to 1932 Malamud attended Erasmus Hall
High School, where he published some stories in *The Erasmian*,
the school's literary magazine. Malamud remembers his high
school English classes as stimulating and awakening, especially
those of Dr. McNeill, chairman of the English Department.
Malamud graduated from New York's City College in 1936
and was awarded his M.A. at Columbia University in 1942;
his thesis was an analysis of Hardy's *The Dynasts*. Malamud's
intention was to teach English in the New York City schools,
but teaching positions were difficult to find in the late days
of the depression so he accepted a federal appointment with
the Bureau of the Census in Washington. Some of his short
prose impressions were published on the contributors' pages
of the Washington *Post*. The story "Girl of My Dreams"
was suggested by an experience he had as an aspiring and
lonely young writer in a strange city.

Returning to New York City and to Erasmus Hall High
School, Malamud taught evening classes in order to have his
days free for writing. He married Ann de Chiara in 1945. In this
period his stories were published in *Threshold* and *American
Preface*. He subsequently held non-teaching positions and
then taught evening classes from 1948 to 1949 at Harlem High
School. Stories such as "Black Is My Favorite Color" and
"Angel Levine" express, one realistically and one in fantasy,
Malamud's life in Brooklyn and his interest in the lives of Jews,
Negroes, Italians, and other minority groups.

He accepted a position in the English Department at Oregon
State College at Corvallis in 1949. Travelling when he was
able and writing stories which appeared in *Harper's Bazaar*,
Partisan Review, *Discovery*, *Commentary*, *The American
Mercury*, *Esquire*, and *New Yorker*, Malamud remained

at Corvallis until 1961. His first novel, *The Natural*, was published in 1952 and dealt with baseball in a combination of fantasy and realism. It received mixed reviews.

In 1956 Malamud received the *Partisan Review* Fiction Fellowship, which enabled him to live in Rome and travel in Europe. The influence of his experiences in Italy can be seen in such stories as "The Maid's Shoes," "The Lady of the Lake," "Behold the Key," and "Naked Nude," which have Italian settings. It is interesting to note that Malamud weaves the past with the present in his work. He gives his mother's maiden name to the American protagonist, Arthur Fidelman, in some of the Italian stories. This Fidelman is also to be the central figure in a projected novel of related short stories.

The Assistant, Malamud's second novel, was published in 1957. It goes back to the gray lives of impoverished shopkeepers in Brooklyn for its characters and setting; but these characters are treated neither in the naturalistic tradition of the proletarian novel of Dreiser and Farrell nor in the sentimental glorification of poverty and simplicity which had become fashionable with the popularity of Steinbeck and Saroyan. For *The Assistant* Malamud received the 1957 Daroff Fiction Award of the Jewish Book Council of America and the 1958 Award of the National Institute of Arts and Letters.

The Magic Barrel, Malamud's first collection of short stories, was published in 1958. The book was widely praised, and reviewers and critics were beginning to pinpoint the distinctive quality of Malamud's approach to his material. For these stories Malamud received the Rosenthal Award of the National Institute of Arts and Letters as well as the National Book Award. In 1959 he was honored also with a Ford Foundation Grant for Creative Writing.

Bennington College, in Vermont, was the setting for the next period of Malamud's life. He became a member of the

Language and Literature Division in 1961, the year in which *A New Life* was published. This novel, which satirically reflects Malamud's Oregon experiences and the impact of the rural West upon his city-conditioned vision, received the most mixed notices of all of his work. It marked a new literary path for Malamud, and judging from its reception, one not without pitfalls.

In 1963 Malamud's short stories appeared in periodicals as diverse as *Commentary* and *Playboy*. This year he was awarded *Playboy*'s annual fiction prize for "Naked Nude," and his second volume of short stories, *Idiots First*, appeared. He was a member of the National Institute of Arts and Letters Book Award Committee which chose Saul Bellow's *Herzog* for its annual award in 1965. He traveled in the Soviet Union, France, and Spain.

The Fixer, published in 1966, differs from Malamud's previous novels in several ways. His only work based upon an actual historical episode, it is a fictionalized version of the Mandel Beiliss case, an infamous example of man's inhumanity to man in the degrading persecution of a Jewish handyman in Czarist Russia. *The Fixer* was reviewed, on several occasions, in conjunction with Maurice Samuel's historical treatment of the same case, *Blood Accusation: The Strange History of the Beiliss Case*, which was published at almost the same time. Both books were praised, although Malamud's work was generally conceded to be the more artistic. For *The Fixer*, he was honored with both the National Book Award and the Pulitzer Prize for Literature. In addition it has been made into a major motion picture.

The Malamud Reader was published late in 1967. Because there was no new work in this volume, its publication elicited no outpouring of reviews and critical estimates of Malamud's work to date. However, several reviewers took the occasion

to write articles placing Malamud with Faulkner and
Hemingway as a major American writer, remarking upon
the variety and virtuosity of his talents.

The critics, on the whole, have been thorough and fair
in evaluating Malamud's work. Because his gift is multi-faceted,
they discuss different aspects of his work. Baumbach discusses
Malamud as fantasist; Bluefarb considers Malamud as
caricaturist and allegorist; Dupee evaluates Malamud as a
realist; Wasserman writes of Malamud as symbolist; Lutz
explores Malamud's "American romanticism"; Rovit treats
of Malamud as a writer in the folk tradition. Predictably,
critics also concern themselves with what they see as Malamud's
shortcomings, what he fails to be, or with what they consider
to be deviations from his true literary path.

The element which makes critical judgment of Malamud
at this time incomplete and possibly grossly inaccurate is the
question of his future writing. Recently he has had stories in
Playboy, The Atlantic, and *Harper's,* and he is currently
completing *Pictures of Fidelman,* a novel of related stories.
Will he write more and finer stories; will he produce the novel
by which our time will be remembered? Was *The Fixer* his
literary peak or was it a false step ... "a soapbox in the public
arena"? Is the story of contemporary issues like "The Man
in the Drawer" a *métier* which Malamud should pursue? He
seems to be enjoying a prolific period, but is his artistry growing
or diminishing?

A bibliography devoted to the work of and about a living
author is necessarily incomplete and inconclusive. This
compilation is offered as an aid to the fascinating pursuit of
reading Malamud's work, considering the criticism, and trying
to reach one's own understanding and conclusions.

In the first section of the checklist the original American
and British publications of Malamud's books have been

documented, and his stories have been traced, as far as possible, to their original appearances with their subsequent collection and reprinting also listed. The second section is divided into three parts: literary criticism in books, in periodicals, and the reviews of each of Malamud's books. British and American sources have been consulted; and the selection comprises articles and reviews in journals of opinion, literary periodicals, both major and local newspapers, religious publications, and periodicals devoted to special interests.

R.K.

Author's Note

This bibliography includes no translated material.
It presents only American and British publication
and critical information.

I wish to thank several persons who have contributed
to the preparation of this paper. Dr. Benjamin Loeb
shared his personal recollection of Malamud; Mr. John
Holland and Miss Leila Karpf of Farrar, Straus and Cudahy
made available reviews and publication information;
and Mr. Diarmiud Russell of Russell and Volkening
provided leads to help in tracing the publication of
the earliest Malamud stories.

Works of Bernard Malamud
Books

A1 *The Natural*. New York: Harcourt, Brace, 1952; London: Eyre and Spottiswoode, 1953.

A2 *The Assistant*. New York: Farrar, Straus and Cudahy, 1957; London: Eyre and Spottiswoode, 1959.

A3 *The Magic Barrel*. New York: Farrar, Straus and Cudahy, 1958; London: Eyre and Spottiswoode, 1960.

Contents: "The First Seven Years"; "The Mourners"; "The Girl of My Dreams"; "Angel Levine"; Behold the Key"; "Take Pity"; "The Prison"; "The Lady of the Lake"; "A Summer's Reading"; "The Bill"; "The Last Mohican"; "The Loan"; "The Magic Barrel."

A4 *A New Life*. New York: Farrar, Straus and Cudahy, 1961; London: Eyre and Spottiswoode, 1962.

A5 *Idiots First*. New York: Farrar, Straus, 1963; London: Eyre and Spottiswoode, 1964.

Contents: "Idiots First"; "Black is My Favorite Color"; "Still Life"; "The Death of Me"; "A Choice of Profession"; "Life Is Better than Death"; "The Jewbird"; Naked Nude"; "The Cost of Living"; "The Maid's Shoes"; "Suppose a Wedding"; "The German Refugee."

A6 *Two Novels by Bernard Malamud, The Natural and The Assistant*. New York: Random House, 1964.

1

2

A7 *The Fixer*. New York: Farrar, Straus and Giroux, 1966; London: Eyre and Spottiswoode, 1967.

A8 *A Malamud Reader*. New York: Farrar, Straus and Giroux, 1967.

Contents: Three Journeys—"To Chicago" (from *The Assistant*, A1); "To the Coast" (from *A New Life*, A4); "To Kiev" (from *The Fixer*, A7). *The Assistant*. In Love and Prison—"S. Levin in Love" (from *A New Life*, A4); "Yakov Bok in Prison" (from *The Fixer*, A7). Stories—"The Mourners"; "The First Seven Years"; "Take Pity"; "The Magic Barrel"; "The Last Mohican" (from *The Magic Barrel*, A3). "Idiots First"; "The Maid's Shoes"; "Black is My Favorite Color"; "The Jewbird"; "The German Refugee" (from *Idiots First*, A5).

Stories

A9 "Benefit Performance," *Threshold*, III (February 1943),
20-22.

A10 "The Place Is Different Now," *American Preface*,
VIII (Spring 1943), 230-242.

A11 "Cost of Living," *Harper's Bazaar*, LXXXIV (March
1950), 142, 209, 212-213. Collected in *Idiots First*, A5.

A12 "The First Seven Years," *Partisan Review*, XVII
(September-October 1950), 661-671. Collected in
The Magic Barrel, A3; *A Malamud Reader*, A8.

A13 "The Prison," *Commentary*, X (September 1950),
252-255. Collected in *The Magic Barrel*, A3. Reprinted
in Martha Foley, ed. *The Best American Short Stories
of 1951*. New York: Houghton Mifflin, 1951, pp.
253-258. In Kenneth Kempton, ed. *Short Stories
for Study*. Cambridge: Harvard University Press, 1953,
pp. 316-321. In Leo Hamalian and Frederick R. Karl,
eds. *The Shape of Fiction: British and American
Short Stories*. New York: McGraw-Hill, 1967, pp.
239-244.

A14 "The Death of Me," *World Review*, XXVI (April
1951), 48-51. Collected in *Idiots First*, A5.

A15 "The Bill," *Commentary*, XI (April 1951), 355-358.
Collected in *The Magic Barrel*, A3.

A16 "An Apology," *Commentary*, XII (November 1951), 460-464.

A17 "The Loan," *Commentary*, XIV (July 1952), 56-59. Collected in *The Magic Barrel*, A3. Reprinted in Norman Podhoretz, ed. *The Commentary Reader*. New York: Atheneum, 1966, pp. 353-358.

A18 "Girl of My Dreams," *American Mercury*, LXXVI (January 1953), 62-71. Collected in *The Magic Barrel*, **A3**.

A19 "The Magic Barrel," *Partisan Review*, XXI (November 1954), 587-603. Collected in *The Magic Barrel*, A3; *A Malamud Reader*, A8. Reprinted in Martha Foley, ed. *The Best American Short Stories of 1955*. New York: Houghton Mifflin, 1955, pp. 169-187. In Herbert Gold, ed. *Fiction of the Fifties*. New York: Doubleday, 1959, pp. 265-283. In Wm. Phillips and Philip Rahv, eds. *The Partisan Review Anthology*. New York: Holt, Rinehart and Winston, 1962, pp. 334-346. In R. W. Lid, ed. *The Short Story, Classic and Contemporary*. New York: Lippincott, 1966, pp. 434-452. In Marcus Klein and Robert Pack, eds. *Short Stories: Classic, Modern, Contemporary*. Boston: Little, Brown, 1967, pp. 498-514. In Mark Schorer, ed. *The Story: A Critical Anthology*. Englewood Cliffs, N.J.: Prentice-Hall, 1967, pp. 122-136. In Lionel Trilling, ed. *The Experience of Literature: Fiction*. New York: Holt, Rinehart and Winston, 1967, pp. 373-385.

A20 "The Mourners," *Discovery*, V (January 1955), 37-95. Collected in *The Magic Barrel*, A3; *A Malamud Reader*, A8. Recorded as read by Bernard Malamud. Boston: Calliope Records, 1963.

A21. "Angel Levine," *Commentary*, xx (December 1955), 534-540. Collected in *The Magic Barrel*, A3. Reprinted in Brom Weber, ed. *An Anthology of American Humor*. New York: Crowell, 1962, pp. 568-577. In J. Leftwich, ed. *Yisroel*. New York: Thomas Yoseloff, 1963, pp. 210-218. In Harry Fenson and Hildreth Kritzer, eds. *Reading, Understanding, and Writing About Short Stories*. New York: Free Press, 1966, pp. 379-389.

A22 "A Summer's Reading," *New Yorker*, xxxii (September 22, 1956), 143-150. Collected in *The Magic Barrel*, A3. Reprinted in Clarence W. Wachner, Frank E. Ross, Eva Marie Van Houten, eds. *Contemporary American Prose*. New York: Macmillan, 1963, pp. 213-220. In M. X. Lesser and John N. Morris, eds. *The Fiction of Experience: Modern Short Stories*. New York: McGraw-Hill, 1962, pp. 404-412. In Robert L. Welker and Herschel Gower, eds. *The Sense of Fiction*. Englewood Cliffs, N.J.: Prentice-Hall, 1966, pp. 155-160.

A23 "The Last Mohican," *Partisan Review*, xxv (Spring 1958), 175-196. Collected in *The Magic Barrel*, A3; *A Malamud Reader*, A8. Reprinted in Martha Foley, ed. *The Best American Short Stories of 1959*. New York: Houghton Mifflin, 1959, pp. 188-208. In Douglas and Sylvia Angus, eds. *Contemporary American Short Stories*. Greenwich, Conn.: Fawcett Publications, 1967, pp. 124-144.

A24 "Behold the Key," *Commentary*, xxv (May 1958), 416-427. Collected in *The Magic Barrel*, A3.

A25 "The Maid's Shoes," *Partisan Review*, xxvi (Winter 1959), 32-44. Collected in *Idiots First*, A5; *A Malamud*

Reader, A8. Reprinted in Martha Foley and David
Burnett, eds. *The Best American Short Stories
of 1960*. New York: Houghton Mifflin, 1960,
pp. 191-204.

A26 "Thanks for Nothing," an excerpt from *A New Life*,
Esquire, LVI (August 1961), 101-112.

A27 "Idiots First," *Commentary*, XXXII (December 1961),
491-496. Collected in *Idiots First*, A5; *A Malamud
Reader*, A8. Reprinted in John Kuehl, ed. *Creative
Writing and Rewriting: Contemporary American
Novelists at Work*. New York: Appleton, 1967,
odd-numbered pages 71-91.

A28 "A Long Ticket for Isaac," early story unpublished until
it appeared in John Kuehl, ed. *Creative Writing
and Rewriting*, Item A27 listed above, even-numbered
pages 70-86.

A29 "Still Life," *Partisan Review*, XXIX (Winter 1962),
95-112. Collected in *Idiots First*, A5.

A30 "Suppose a Wedding," *New Statesman*, LXV (February
8, 1963), 198-200. Collected in *Idiots First*, A5.

A31 "The Jewbird," *Reporter*, XXVIII (April 11, 1963),
33-36. Collected in *Idiots First*, A5; *A Malamud Reader*,
A8. Reprinted in Richard Poirier, ed. *Prize Stories,
1963-1964: The O. Henry Awards*. New York:
Doubleday, 1964, pp. 60-79. In James B. Hall, ed.
The Realm of Fiction: Sixty-one Short Stories. New York:
McGraw-Hill, 1965, pp. 393-401.

A32 "Life Is Better than Death," *Esquire*, LIX (May 1963),
78-79. Collected in *Idiots First*, A5.

A33 "Naked Nude," *Playboy*, x (August 1963), 48-50,
52, 122-124. Collected in *Idiots First*, A5. Reprinted
in Hugh M. Hefner, ed. *The Twelfth Anniversary
Playboy Reader*. Chicago: *Playboy* Press, 1965, pp. 12-27.

A34 "Black Is My Favorite Color," *Reporter*, xxix
(July 18, 1963), 43-44. Collected in *Idiots First*, A5;
A Malamud Reader, A8.

A35 "The Refugee," *Saturday Evening Post*, ccxxxvi
(September 14, 1963), 38-39. Collected in *Idiots First*, A5;
A Malamud Reader, A8.

A36 "Choice of Profession," *Commentary*, xxxvi
(September 1963), 235-241. Collected in *Idiots First*,
A5.

A37 "Take Pity." In *The Magic Barrel*, A3. Reprinted in
Robert Gordon, ed. *The Expanded Moment*. Boston:
Heath, 1963, pp. 91-98. In Irving Malin and Irwin Stark,
eds. *Breakthrough: A Treasury of Contemporary
American-Jewish Literature*. New York: McGraw-Hill,
1964, pp. 87-94. In Eugene Cuirent-Garcia and Walton
R. Patrick, eds. *American Short Stories*. Chicago:
Scott, Foresman, 1964, pp. 534-542. In Arthur Mizener, ed.
Modern Short Stories: the Uses of Imagination. New
York: Norton, 1967, pp. 526-535. Collected in
The Malamud Reader, A8.

A38 "A Pimp's Revenge," *Playboy*, xiv (February 1968),
68-70, 126, 156.

A39 "Man in the Drawer," *Atlantic*, ccxxi (April 1968),
70-78, 83-93.

A40 "Pictures of Fidelman," *Atlantic*, CCXXII (December 1968), 63-70.

A41 "An Exorcism," *Harper's*, CCXXXVII (December 1968), 76-89.

Secondary Sources
Criticism in Books

B1 Aldridge, John W. "Notes on the Novel II." In his *Time to Murder and Create: The Contemporary Novel in Crisis*. New York: McKay, 1966, pp. 53-94.

"Perhaps . . . boredom, this curious double sense of irrelevance and predictability, accounts for the fact that, although they appear to hold [Bellow and Malamud, or Baldwin and Mailer] in the highest esteem, our literary intellectuals do not customarily look to them to provide the basic terms for understanding or evaluating the experience of the present age."

B2 Allen, Walter. *The Modern Novel in Britain and the United States*. New York: E. P. Dutton, 1964, pp. 322, 330-332.

"Bellow and Malamud have brought a new note into the American novel. It is Jewish certainly but also . . . Russian . . . which shows that American fiction is still capable of sudden growth, development, and expansion in directions scarcely predictable."

B3 Baumbach, Jonathan. "All Men Are Jews: Three Novels by Bernard Malamud." In his *The Landscape of Nightmare*. New York: N.Y.U. Press, 1965, pp. 101-122.

This is a slight reworking of Baumbach's *Kenyon Review* article, Item B30.

9

B4 Burgess, Anthony. "American Themes." In his *The Novel Now: A Guide to Contemporary Fiction*. New York: Norton, 1967, pp. 197-198.

"In many ways [Malamud's novels] are more traditional than either Bellow's or Gold's, showing a kinship with the older Yiddish literature, in which the world of spirit impinges on that of the flesh and, without surprise, we see the supernatural (disguised as surrealism) closing in, the world of objects dissolving, the very identities of people becoming unsure."

B5 Dupee, F.W. "Malamud: the Uses and Abuses of Commitment." In his *The King of the Cats*, New York: Farrar, Straus and Giroux, 1965, pp. 156-163.

This is a reprint of Dupee's review of *Idiots First*, Item B161.

B6 Fiedler, Leslie A. *Love and Death in the American Novel*. New York: Criterion, 1960, pp. 469-470.

"Freer [than Rosenfeld and Goodman] in creating a full-scale novel in the Kafkaesque mode and the Surrealist tradition is Bernard Malamud . . . in *The Natural* . . . which creates a magical universe . . . with lovely absurd madness."

B7 ————. "Three Jews," in *NO! in Thunder*. Boston: Beacon Press, 1960, pp. 101-110.

This is a reprint of Fiedler's reviews of *The Natural* and *The Assistant*, Items B78 and B93.

B8 ————. "Jewish Americans Go Home!" In his *Waiting for the End*. New York: Stein and Day, 1964, pp. 89-104.

"Even more daring, and finally, I think, more successful, is Malamud's attempt in *The Assistant* to create a Jewish Gentile . . . a man who moves from a position of vague hostility to the Jews, through exclusion and suffering, to the point where he is ready to accept circumcision—to become *de jure* what he is already *de facto*, one of the ultimately insulted and

injured, a Jew. . . . It is one of the oldest and . . . most
unforeseen happy endings . . . and it could only have happened
in 1957, at the high point of the movement [of American
identification with the Jew.]"

B9 Hassan, Ihab. "The Qualified Encounter." In his *Radical
Innocence: The Contemporary American Novel.*
Princeton: Princeton University Press, 1961, pp. 161-168.

"The first and most obvious quality of his fiction is its
'goodness.' This is a complex quality compounded of irony,
trust, and craft—a touch of Dostoevski and Chagall . . . deeply
responsible to its feeling of what transforms a man into
mensch."

B10 Hicks, Granville. "Generation of the Fifties: Malamud,
Gold, and Updike." In Nona Balakian and Charles
Simmons, eds. *The Creative Present.* New York:
Doubleday, 1963, pp. 217-237.

"Perhaps it is worth noting that [Malamud's heroes] have been
thrust alone into a world they could not conceive of
making. . . . Malamud is looking for a path [for the redemption
of the individual] and convinces us, by the power of his
imagination, that paths can be found."

B11 Hoffman, Frederick J. "Marginal Societies in the Novel."
In his *The Modern Novel in America.* Chicago: Henry
Regnery, 1963, pp. 224-255.

"*The Assistant* is especially representative of Malamud's skill
in exploiting the ultimate possibilities of Jewish suffering
and the pain of relations with the *goyim.* . . . The important
facts come from the use of Jewish manners . . . which are
based upon essential Jewish religious qualities and form of
meditation. . . ."

B12 Hoyt, C. A. "Bernard Malamud and the New
Romanticism." In Harry T. Moore, ed. *Contemporary*

American Novelists. Carbondale: S. Illinois U. Press, 1964, pp. 65-79.

"The suffering of the Jews is to Bernard Malamud the stuff and substance of his art; from it he has fashioned works of surpassing beauty and integrity and a sure place among the best writers of his time."

B13 Hyman, Stanley Edgar. "A New Life for a Good Man." In his *Standards: A Chronicle of Books for Our Time.* New York: Horizon, 1967, pp. 33-37.

B14 ————. "A New Life for a Good Man." In Richard Kostelanetz, ed. *On Contemporary Literature.* New York: Avon, 1964, pp. 442-446.

B13 and B14 are reprints of Hyman's *New Leader* review of *A New Life,* Item B143.

B15 Kazin, Alfred. "Bernard Malamud: The Magic and the Dread." In his *Contemporaries.* Boston: Little, Brown, 1962, pp. 202-207.

"Malamud's world has its own haunting archetypes . . . its tense expressiveness is one of the cultural symbols of the Jews, in art as in religion . . . Malamud captures the strangeness of Jewish experience brilliantly . . . comes close to the bone of human feeling."

B16 ————. "Bernard Malamud: The Magic and the Dread." In Richard Kostelanetz, ed. *On Contemporary Literature.* New York: Avon, 1964, pp. 437-441.

This is a reprint of Item B15.

B17 Kempton, Kenneth Payson. "For Plot Read Idea." In his *Short Stories for Study.* Cambridge: Harvard University Press, 1953, pp. 316-321.

In a discussion of the element of plot in the short story, Kempton uses "The Prison" to exemplify the story in which

the "pattern of action was not ferreted out as a separate entity,
an end in itself, and the characters pushed into enacting it.
'The Prison' appears to have followed naturally upon the
author's discovery of two persons capable of illustrating
a tenable idea."

B18 Klein, Marcus. "Bernard Malamud: The Sadness of
Goodness." In his *After Alienation*. Cleveland: World
Publishing Co., 1962, pp. 247-293.

"The radiant artifacts of Bernard Malamud's fiction have been
the shrouds and graves of Jews: rusty caftans and rusty black
derbies, decrepit tenements, gloomy grocery stores smelling
of poverty, of age, and of inviolate failure ... the Jewish
community . . . which has traditionally denied the priority
of existence, has been the constant condition of his sensibility."

B19 Kuehl, John. "Characterization and Structure." In his
*Creative Writing and Rewriting: Contemporary
American Novelists at Work*. New York:
Appleton, 1967, pp. 70-92.

Kuehl contrasts the early Malamud story, "A Long Ticket
for Isaac" with the published story, "Idiots First." Both stories treat,
to some extent, the theme of Abraham's sacrifice of Isaac.
The stories appear on facing pages in the book. The published
story ["Barrel"], says Malamud, is "a better piece of work"
than the "unsuccessful" earlier draft. Kuehl says it "attains
better organization and presents more subtly and complexly
the [main] characters."

B20 Ludwig, Jack. *Recent American Novelists*. Minneapolis:
U. of Minnesota Press, 1962, pp. 39-41.

"A similar progression [a fear not only of being identified with
but of being permanently fixed in a region or a cause]
is observable in the work of Malamud, like Bellow . . . a
celebrator of the Jew in America."

B21 Malamud, Bernard. "Address from the Fiction Winner."
In John Fisher and Robert B. Silvers, eds. *Writing
in America*. New Brunswick, N.J.: Rutgers University
Press, 1960, p. 173.

Malamud's address is printed in its entirety. This excerpt
expresses his literary credo:

"It seems to me that the writer's most important task, no matter
what the current theory of man, or his prevailing mood, is to
recapture his image as human being as each of us in his secret heart
knows it to be, and as history and literature have from the
beginning revealed it."

B22 Malin, Irving. *Jews and Americans*. Carbondale and
Edwardsville: Southern Illinois University Press, 1965.

This study measures Malamud and six other American Jewish
writers against a variety of themes having to do with
Jewishness. "Laughter and trembling, the intermingling of
'Is and Ought'—such ironic dualities appear in Malamud's
fiction."

B23 ———— and Irvin Stark. Introduction to *Breakthrough:
A Treasury of Contemporary American-Jewish
Literature*. New York: McGraw-Hill, 1964, p. 20.

"The theme of suffering, which runs through American-Jewish
fiction, has been exploited most effectively by Bernard
Malamud."

B24 Richman, Sidney. *Bernard Malamud*. New York:
Twayne, 1966.

This is a 145-page book devoted to discussion and appraisal of
Malamud's achievement, considering the short stories and
novels written prior to *The Fixer*. Helpful notes and a short
selected bibliography are included.

B25 Siegel, Ben. "Victims in Motion: Bernard Malamud's
Sad and Bitter Clowns."

In J. J. Waldmeir, ed. *Recent American Fiction*. Boston: Houghton-Mifflin, 1963, pp. 203-214.

Reprint of Siegel's article in *The Northwest Review*, Item B69.

B26 Trilling, Lionel. Comments on 'The Magic Barrel.' In his *The Experience of Literature: Fiction*. New York: Holt, 1967, pp. 371-373.

"Much of the curious power and charm of "The Magic Barrel" is . . . the extraordinary visual intensity of the last [paragraph] but one. . . . The intense pictorial quality . . . is . . . a reminiscence of the iconography of . . . Marc Chagall. . . . Chagall [and Malamud] depict with . . . reverence the religious life . . . but . . . love is marked not only by the joy that is natural to it but also by the joy of its liberation from the piety that had held it in check."

B27 Ulanov, Barry. "The Short Story," "The Novel," in *The Two Worlds of American Art: The Private and the Popular*, New York: Macmillan, 1965, pp. 205, 232-233.

Malamud is cited as one of "a new group of short-story writers not ashamed to make special pleas. . . . Irony . . . is invariably present. . . . Malamud's . . . happy-unhappy protagonists and antagonists [are seen as] . . . closely related in simple, not quite sober resignation to the people of Sholom Aleichem."

"Malamud chooses feeling above all in *The Assistant* [which is] closer to the better writers for the Yiddish theater than is Chagall." Ulanov prefers *The Assistant* to *The Natural* and *A New Life*.

Criticism in Periodicals

B28 "A Talk with Bernard Malamud," New York *Times Book Review*, October 8, 1961, p. 28.

> "Lacking the one and not being the other, Bernard Malamud will disclaim connection with the bearded S. Levin, former drunkard, who gets off the transcontinental train to give *A New Life* one of the most splendid opening paragraphs of the year."

B29 Adler, Dick. "The Magician of 86 Street," *Book World*, October 29, 1967, p. 8.

> "My opinion is that [Bellow, Roth, Malamud] are American writers who happen to be Jewish. . . . To me, a Jewish writer is a man who is immersed in Jewishness."

B30 Baumbach, Jonathan. "The Economy of Love: the Novels of Bernard Malamud," *Kenyon Review*, XXV (Summer 1963), 438-457.

> Malamud is a "moral fabler and fantasist" whose novels all deal with the "broken dreams and private griefs of the spirit" and the "redemptive power and tragic defeat of love. . . . Love is sacred in Malamud's universe; if life is holy, love is a holy of holies." Reprinted in B3.

B31 ————. "Malamud's Heroes," *Commonweal*, LXXXV (October 28, 1966), 97-99.

> "Malamud is a didactic writer, a moralist. . . . He dreams the dream of our failed heroism and conceives us better men for having risked defeat. . . . a brave book!"

B32 Bellman, Samuel Irving. "Women, Children, and Idiots First: the Transformation Psychology of Bernard Malamud," *Critique*, VII (Winter 1964-1965), 123-138.

Many of Malamud's characters "find the world unfit to live in, but for a few a new life is possible."

B33 Bluefarb, Sam. "Bernard Malamud: the Scope of Caricature," *English Journal*, XXIII (July 1964), 319-326.

"Malamud's caricatures frequently attain allegorical significance . . ." and some Malamud characters are cited to substantiate this observation.

B34 "Books They Liked Best," *Book World*, December 3, 1967, p. 6.

In an article in which literary luminaries selected their favorite reading in 1967, Bernard Malamud chose *A Personal Anthology* by Jorge Luis Borges, *The Autobiography of Bertrand Russell, 1872-1914*, and *Mr. Clemens and Mark Twain*, by Justin Kaplan.

B35 Cadle, Dean. "Bernard Malamud," *Wilson Library Bulletin*, XXXIII (December 1958) 266.

In a detailed biographical sketch, Bernard Malamud is quoted as saying, "Our fiction is loaded with sickness, homosexuality, fragmented man, 'other-directed' man. It should be filled with love and beauty and hope. We are underselling man."

B36 Charles, Gerda. "Bernard Malamud — the 'Natural' Writer," *Jewish Quarterly*, IX (Spring, 1962), pp. 5-6.

The Natural and several short stories in *The Magic Barrel* have "an uncanny quality. . . . even the sometimes vulgar *A New Life* has more depth than Kingsley Amis's *Lucky Jim.* . . ."

B37 Edelstein, J.M. "Binding Variants in Malamud's *The Natural*," *American Notes and Queries*, I (May 1963), 133-134.

"Copies of the first edition of . . . *The Natural* . . . have been recorded in three variations in the color of the buckram binding. . . . The records of the publication do not show any distinction among these colors, but only that the first printing was larger than had been anticipated, which may have necessitated using whatever colors were at hand."

B38 Featherstone, Joseph. "Bernard Malamud," *Atlantic*, CCXIX (March 1967), 95-98.

"Like the great Yiddish writer Isaac Bashevis Singer, Malamud is fascinated by the intersection of the commonplace and the comic grotesque, the grotesque being a metaphor for a particular sense of dislocation that pervades his work. . . . *The Assistant*, his masterpiece so far, is surely one of the finest novels of the decade. . . . *The Natural* and the weaker new novel, *The Fixer*, reveal an excess of intent, a desire to do things on a grand scale that is not altogether fruitful. Still, as one of the country's most accomplished writers, he has earned the right to gamble on his ambition."

B39 Francis, H.E. "Bernard Malamud's Everyman," *Midstream*, VII (Winter 1961), 93-97.

"Though doctrine immediately defines [Malamud's] characters, compassion ultimately does so. For it is compassion, not theology, which allies his Christian and Jewish characters."

B40 Frankel, Haskel. "Interview with Bernard Malamud," *Saturday Review*, IX (September 10, 1966) 39, 40.

Malamud is quoted as saying, "My work, all of it, is an idea of dedication to the human."

B41 Geismar, Maxwell. "The American Short Story Today," *Studies on the Left*, IV (Spring 1964), 21-27.

Contemporary American writers like J. Updike, J. D. Salinger,

and Bernard Malamud . . . are "too successfully adjusted to
their present fame and fortune to break through their own
literary mode."

B42 ————. "The Jewish Heritage in Contemporary
American Fiction," *Ramparts*, II (Autumn 1963) 5-13.

"The humor of the outcast and . . . the complacency of the
anointed live side by side as attempts of recent Jewish novelists
to reconstruct the values of their disappearing heritage."

B43 Glanville, Brian. "The Sporting Novel," New York
Times Book Review, July 18, 1965, p. 2.

"The sporting novel . . . must either be proletarian or a fantasy;
either a *This Sporting Life* [by David Storey] or *The
Natural.* . . . In *The Natural*, [Malamud] divines the
unconscious need, both collective and individual, which has
made professional sport possible and necessary, and has
created its heroes and its legends. . . . Thus, whether Malamud
has the detail of the baseball world right is beside the point.
The book is true in terms of myth, in terms of the
compensatory function which all professional sport fulfills
in our tame, urbanized experience."

B44 Goldman, Mark. "Bernard Malamud's Comic Vision and
the Theme of Identity," *Critique*, VII
(Winter 1964-65), 92-109.

Malamud's works are more than chronicles of Jewish life. . . .
His "mood is wide-ranging but his theme is consistently
the individual's need for suffering to attain self-knowledge."

B45 Gross, John. "Marjorie Morningstar, Ph.D," *New
Statesman*, LXIV (November 30, 1962), 921.

Malamud and Bellow present "the intensity of the past entering
into an ambiguous relationship to present Jewish society. . . .
while Roth belongs with slick professionals."

B46 Guerin, Ann. "The Tormented Tale of an Innocent,"
Life, LXIV (February 16, 1968), 88-92.

This is a pictorial description of the filming of *The Fixer* in
a village in Communist Hungary which has been altered
to resemble Kiev in the early years of the twentieth century,
when the Beiliss case took place.

B47 Hassan, Ihab. "The Way Down and Out," *Virginia
Quarterly Review*, XXXIX (Winter 1963), 81-93.

"The shudder of 'deflection,' the spiritual gesture of disavowal
of evil without confidence in good, is found in the 'Christlike
martyr' . . . in Bernard Malamud."

B48 Hicks, Granville. "American Fiction in 1958," *Saturday
Review*, XLI (December 27, 1958), 12.

"Of the collection of short stories I read [in 1958] the finest
was Bernard Malamud's *The Magic Barrel* with its gentle
tales of suffering and guilt."

B49 —————. "His Hopes on the Human Heart," *Saturday
Review* XLVI (October 12, 1963), 31-32.

Sketches Malamud's career to date . . . "He has been greatly
troubled by the depreciation of the human in modern
times. . . . He believes that the human must be protected and the
note he sounds again and again is compassion."

B50 Hogan, William. "Bernard Malamud's 'Gallows
Humor,' " San Francisco *Chronicle*, (October 25, 1963),
23.

"Malamud documents the drama of loneliness . . . makes
a profound point with merely a shrug or a grin."

B51 Howe, Irving. "Mass Society and Post-Modern Fiction,"
Partisan Review, XXVI (Summer 1959), 420-436.

The recent novelist [Malamud and others] must find new ways

to test character, so he approaches American life obliquely, using as his subject the 'marginal, the off-beat.' "

B52 Hruska, Richard J. "My Grandfather and Morris Bober," *C.C.C.: The Journal of the Conference on College Composition and Communication*, XIII (May 1962), 32-34.

In this discussion of the novel, Hruska, a student, writes that Morris Bober in *The Assistant* "died believing he was a failure" . . . although the persons who had once deceived him now "admired his personal integrity." He never understands that his method brought him admiration.

B53 Jones, G. William. "Current Novelists and 'Entering into the World,' " *Southwest Review*, XLIX (Winter 1964-65), 91-96.

"These [*Idiots First*] are stories of love that reaches out in tenderness and gets its hands frozen off."

B54 Kauffmann, Stanley. "Greatness as a Literary Standard," *Harper's*, CCXXXI (November 1965), 151-156.

Idiots First, among other works, is cited as an example of highest American literary achievement.

B55 ————. "Some of Our Best Writers," *Review of Jews and Americans* by Irving Malin. New York *Times Book Review*, May 30, 1965, 1, 16, 18.

Kauffmann says Malin (See Item B22) measures Malamud and other American-Jewish writers against "a Procrustean bed of Jewishness."

B56 Leer, Norman, "Escape and Confrontation in the Short Stories of Philip Roth," *Christian Scholar*, XLVIII (Fall 1965), 132-146.

Roth is described as feeling that in his stories he has forced upon society "an awareness of reality," while he (Roth) criticizes Salinger, Malamud, and Bellow for "their avoidance of direct encounter with the American complexity."

B57 ————. "Three American Novels and Contemporary Society," *Wisconsin Studies in Contemporary Literature*, III (Fall 1962), 67-86.

". . . *The Assistant* emphasizes the condition of alienation within social interaction, and the need to realize and be able to fulfill some obligation to others. . . . Both a part of and set apart from 'mass society,' [Malamud's characters] must begin further back and find roles to which their heroic dreams can apply."

B58 Mandel, Ruth B. "Bernard Malamud's *The Assistant* and *A New Life*: Ironic Affirmation," *Critique*, VIII (Winter 1964-1965), 110-122.

The essay examines *The Assistant* and *A New Life* to show the personal search for values each recounts. The latter novel is deemed inferior "because of its attempted social criticism."

B59 Marcus, Steven. "The Novel Again," *Partisan Review*, XXIX (Spring 1962), 171-195.

The novel in the last fifteen years has declined "from novelistic to poetic forms," as evidenced in work of William Golding and Bernard Malamud, and has lost the assumption of "a future of development and change."
In America, Bernard Malamud exemplifies the tendencies to bring " . . . conscious and unconscious processes simultaneously before the reader, and for rendering past and present as co-existent." All of his novels to date are "mystical . . . about the experience of rebirth; in each of them a prematurely oldish young man . . . is given a second chance to make something of himself and redeem his disreputable past."

B60 Mollard, James M. "Malamud's Novels: Four Versions of Pastoral," *Critique*, IX (1967), 5-19.

"For Malamud the pastoral mode [which lacks realistic specificity] is his greatest strength as a writer of fiction, because it has given him an archetypal convention of characterization, a consistent pattern of imagery, a durable convention of characterization, and a style and rhetorical strategy of lucidity and power. Although Malamud employs different versions of pastoral in each novel, *The Fixer* . . . pushes the mode into areas never quite reached in [his earlier novels]."

B61 Meras, Phyllis. "An Interview with Bernard Malamud," Providence *Sunday Journal*, September 11, 1966, H-9.

In an interview Malamud speaks about the sources of ideas and inspiration for his novels. *The Fixer*, he says, is based upon "an idea carried around from Russia in my father's memory."

B62 Mudrick, Marvin. "Who Killed Herzog? or, Three American Novelists," *Denver Quarterly*, I (Spring 1966), 61-97.

"Malamud, Bellow, and Roth have taken upon themselves the job of inventing the contemporary fictional Jew."

B63 Perrine, Lawrence. "Malamud's 'Take Pity,' " *Studies in Short Fiction*, II (Fall 1964) 84-86.

The theme of "Take Pity" depends upon correct identification of its setting, not as hell exactly, but as "a kind of purgatory which Malamud creates somewhere in outer space. . . . Rosen has committed suicide. . . . The theme of the story . . . is concerned with the tangled human emotions of pity and pride."

B64 Podhoretz, Norman. "The New Nihilism in the American Novel," *Partisan Review*, XXV (Fall 1958), 589-590.

"The trick [Malamud] has turned is not unlike what Yeats did with magic: in the absence of a culture that could supply him with the things he needs to believe, he has created a folk partly out of what actually exists and partly out of what his spirit demands. You would not go to [him] for a . . .

reliable picture of the East European immigrant Jew, but . . . for profounder truths about human beings than mere observation can yield."

B65 Pritchett, V.S. "That Time and That Wilderness," *New Statesman*, LXIV (September 28, 1962), 405-406.

"For Malamud and Bellow . . . inhabited America is non-existent" and life is an abstraction, as contrasted to Faulkner, who creates a South in depth.

B66 Ratner, Marc L. "Style and Humanity in Malamud's Fiction," *Massachusetts Review*, V (Summer 1964), 663-683.

"Malamud's style and variety of subject have not been sufficiently appreciated; his ironic but humanistic view of life is well served by his creative and eclectic style."

B67 Rovit, Earl H. "Bernard Malamud and the Jewish Literary Tradition," *Critique*, III (Winter-Spring 1960), 3-10.

Although Malamud works within the tradition of Yiddish folklore and vignette, his structural mode is "poetic and symbolic, resolving unresolvable conflicts in images of deliberate ambiguity. . . . His restrictive irony may be a limitation of his art."

B68 Shear, Walter. "Culture Conflicts in *The Assistant*," *The Midwest Quarterly*, VII (Summer 1966), 367-380.

"In *The Assistant*, two cultures, the Jewish tradition and the American heritage (representing the wisdom of the old world and the practical knowledge of the new), collide and to some degree synthesize to provide a fixture of social documentation which is manifested in a realistic aesthetic. . . . Man, caught between the conflicting claims of cultural values, suffers not only because of his circumstances but because a fragmented abundance of world views produces uncertainty about intentions, actions, and roles."

B69 Siegel, Ben. "Victims in Motion: Bernard Malamud's
Sad and Bitter Clowns," *Northwest Review*, v
(Spring, 1962), 69-80.

Each of Malamud's works . . . "is a moral critique, an attempt
to explore and reveal the melancholic state of the human
condition, its basic—even banal realities. . . . [He gives] an
ironic yet compassionate insight into the dark dilemma
that is modern life."

B70 Sheppard, Ronald Z. "About Bernard Malamud,"
Washington *Post*, October 13, 1963, 5.

Malamud is quoted as explaining that the main theme of his
work is the "development of the hidden strengths of
ordinary and often awkward people."

B71 Solotaroff, Theodore. "Roth and the Jewish Moralists,"
Chicago *Review*, xiii (Winter 1959), 87-99.

In an essay in which Philip Roth is compared and contrasted
with other American-Jewish writers, Solotaroff says Roth
"resembles Malamud . . . in the moral intention."

B72 "Sustaining Stream," *Time*, lxxxi (February 1,
1963) 84.

In "a recommended reading list of ten American novelists
whose first work appeared within the last few years," Bernard
Malamud is described as dancing "a fine step on the wavy
line between myth and mundanity. . . . [He] has subtly shifted
reality, as a dream peddler must, to suit the thread of his
dream."

B73 Wasserman, Earl R. *"The Natural*: Malamud's World
Ceres," *Centennial Review of Arts and Sciences*,
ix (Fall 1965), 438-460.

"Baseball has given Malamud a ritualistic system that cuts
across all our regional and social differences in *The Natural* . . .
[*The Natural*] is the broad formulation of Malamud's world

of meaning for in it he evolved the structure of symbols
and the design of thematic patterns and relationships on which
he has drawn in *The Assistant* and *A New Life*."

B74 Weiss, Samuel A. "Notes on Bernard Malamud,"
Chicago Jewish Forum, XXI (Winter 1962-1963),
155-158.

Malamud's hero is bound to the Dostoevskian cult of
suffering and martyrdom. . . . The candle of morality burns . . .
but its light is cold and abstract in his consciousness and
leaves his deeper motivations in the dark."

B75 Wershba, Joe. "Not Horror but 'Sadness,' " New York
Post, September 14, 1958, p. M-2.

In an interview in which biographical background is presented,
Malamud describes all of his fiction as telling the story of
"personality fulfilling itself."

B76 White, Robert L. "The English Instructor as Hero . . .
Two Novels by Roth and Malamud," *Forum*
(University of Houston), IV (Winter 1963), 16-22.

Malamud in *A New Life* examines "American culture in
general" and deals extensively with the academic world. The
novel is limited, however, because it is restricted to a
homogeneous, although not strictly "Jewish subject matter and
society."

Book Reviews

The Natural

B77 Brooke, Jocelyn, *The Listener*, LXIX (May 9, 1963), 801.

"I find it hard to understand where the [Homeric] heroism comes in, for it seems to me that a brainless and amoral lout, possessed by an overweening ambition to be the world's greatest baseball player, can hardly qualify for heroic status. Mr. Malamud . . . has me baffled."

B78 Fiedler, Leslie A. "In the Interest of Surprise and Delight," *Folio*, XX (Summer 1955), 17-20.

"The ball team of *The Natural* is real . . . but behind the literal fable, there is the presence of a legend . . . the Grail legend. Mr. Malamud reaches out with one hand to Ring Lardner and with the other to Jessie Weston." Reprinted in B7.

B79 Fitzgerald, E. J. *Saturday Review*, XXXV (September 6, 1952), 32.

"Bernard Malamud has taken some potentially exciting material and gone all mystical and cosmic on it with somewhat unhappy results. . . . Despite some sharp observations, nice sardonic touches . . . he doesn't quite bring it off."

B80 Henderson, R.W. *Library Journal*, LXXVII (September 1, 1952), 1.

"A sardonic view of players and fans. For mature readers."

B81 Igoe, William J. "More Than One America", *The Tablet*, CCXVII (May 11, 1963), 513.

> "Mr. Malamud is one of the half dozen great short story writers in the language. Like Mr. O'Connor he has the advantage of being a member of a minority formed by persecutions. . . . *The Natural*, a young man's novel, written before he discovered the Jews, is a discovery of America . . . romance shot through with satire reminiscent of Nathanael West. . . . written out of a sad enchantment that is beautifully American."

B82 *Kirkus Bulletin*, XX (July 15, 1952), 420.

> "A strange and arresting story which men, even those who never get further than the newspaper, should enjoy."

B83 Lodge, David. "Home Run," *Spectator*, (May 10, 1963), 608, 610.

> "By treating his subject mythopoeically, Malamud gives a new beauty and nobility to the athletic drama without sacrificing any excitement."

B84 Maloney, J. J. New York *Herald Tribune Book Review*, August 24, 1952, p. 8.

> "Bernard Malamud's novel is a troubled mixture of fantasy and realism in which the fantasy is fantastic enough, but the realism is not very real."

B85 Miller, Karl. "Sporting Life," *New Statesman*, LXV (April 19, 1963), 602.

> "This is an elegant, ethereal book, the wonderful inauguration of a very gifted writer. He writes like a scholar gypsy, a triumphant hybrid style."

B86 *New Yorker*, XXVIII (September 6, 1952), 117.

> "A book about a baseball player, related in a thin and ingenuous voice that seems to indicate that the writer would like us to search beneath the surface of his story for the meanings he has hidden there."

B87 Podhoretz, Norman, "Achilles in Left Field,"
Commentary, xv (March 1963), 321-326.

" . . . The appearance of an intelligent novelist who finds it
possible to say something about a popular 'mass' phenomenon
through the medium of a popular literary form is a very
healthy sign. . . . nevertheless . . . he does not succeed in
achieving that synthesis of the pop and the serious for which he
aims."

B88 Price, R. G. G. *Punch*, ccxliv (May 1, 1963), 645.

It is supposed to be an allegory . . . and "the last reaction the
writer of allegory should produce is, 'So what!' "

B89 Ross, Alan, *London Magazine*, iii (June 1963), 86.

"It would seem that Malamud wrote *The Natural* after a heavy
bout of Nathanael West. . . . This is a poet's book, far
removed from Lardner's and Runyon's comic eccentrics, for it
has a depth of feeling and a lyrical, almost balletic
progression that survives its improbability and melodrama. . . .
[It] provides an exciting first glimpse of a remarkable writer
tackling the steepest route to the summit."

B90 Sylvester, Harry, New York *Times Book Review*,
August 24, 1952, 5.

" . . . an unusually fine novel. . . . A sustained and elaborate
allegory in which the 'natural' player . . . is equated with
the natural man. . . . A brilliant and unusual book."

The Assistant

B91 Barley, Anthony. "Insidious Patience," *Commonweal*,
lxvi (June 21, 1957), 307-308.

"It is one of Malamud's chief merits that he hews a strict and
narrow path between the Scylla of indiscreet affirmation . . .
and the Charybdis of sentimental poverty . . . the morality,
like the style . . . is a surprise . . . unexpected but perfectly
right."

B92 Butz, R. C. San Francisco *Chronicle*, May 16, 1957, p. 29.

"There is a binding theme throughout the book, a search for
fundamental truths through the study of ordinary people,
their everyday ups and downs, their mundane pleasures and
pains. . . . Malamud's vision, style, and world are
distinctively original."

B93 Fiedler, Leslie A. "The Commonplace as Absurd,"
Reconstructionist, XXIV (February 21, 1958), 22-24.

"*The Assistant* treats gray lives grayly . . . but the poetry is
never denied. Malamud has chosen to create the least
melodramatic of all possible versions of the Absurd: a
vision of the commonplace as absurd." Reprinted in B7.

B94 Friedman, Robert. "Passion and Groceries," St. Louis
Post-Dispatch, June 13, 1957, p.21

"It is . . . to the author's credit that he is able to construct a story
of such outright power and impact in a milk-bottle nickel-and-
dime setting. . . . He uses the . . . drabness of the background
to heighten the effect of the story. He asserts (by extension)
that human conflict and passion are not measured by the roof
under which they stir and rise . . ."

B95 Gold, Herbert. *The Nation*, CLXXXIV (April 20, 1957),
350.

"*The Assistant* is almost perfect as far as it goes. In his work to
come, it will be important for Malamud to take some chances
on the wit and the love of life which he gives us so far in a
minor key. [His work is] lyric marvels—the headlong
architectural daring of a great novelist."

B96 Goyen, William. "A World of Bad Luck," New York
Times Book Review, April 28, 1957, p. 4.

"Mr. Malamud's people are memorable and real as rock, and
there is not one gesture of sentimentality or theatrics to
render them so."

B97 Hayes, E. Nelson. *The Progressive*, XXI (July 1957), 29.

The Assistant "is a tender novel about little people. . . . It tells a story of subtle ironies and many levels. . . . Malamud writes convincingly and compassionately of his people; he is a stylist who fuses material and theme and language into a meaningful unity of deep sincerity."

B98 Hicks, Granville. "A Note on Literary Journalism and Good Novels by Moore and Malamud," *The New Leader*, XL (April 29, 1957), 21-22.

The Assistant is " . . . a somber, meticulous examination of the complexity of human maturation. . . . It has neither the extravagance nor the humor of . . . [*The Natural*]. On the contrary, the material is familiar and the tone quiet. . . . I found myself more and more deeply involved. . . . [Unlike] Depression novels that were written in the thirties, the [characters'] predicaments are not blamed by them or by the author on . . . social conditions. Malamud's attention is focused on psychological, ethical, and religious problems. . . . He has a strong grasp on the problems that concern him and writes about them with admirable insight."

B99 Kazin, Alfred. "Fantasist of the Ordinary," *Commentary*, XXIV (July 1957), 89-92.

"Malamud is the poet of the desperately clownish, not of the good who shall inherit the earth. . . . He writes, a little, the way Chagall paints."

B100 Kilby, C. S. New York *Herald Tribune Book Review*, April 28, 1957, p. 8.

"The plot is lightly knit, the characters true, and the meaning eminently worthwhile."

B101 *Kirkus Bulletin*, XXV (February 1, 1957), 101.

"Despite its occasional spark of humanity and its melancholy humor, this is on the whole too grim a picture to have wide appeal."

B102 Levin, Meyer. *Saturday Review*, XL (June 15, 1957), 21.

"Malamud creates an amazing tension in his story of the
growth of conscience. He keeps the tale refined down to
essential scenes, in the manner of the newer novelists who work
carefully in a defined frame, revealing with intensity the
personal tales of a small cast of characters. He is a writer who
certainly will count amongst the literary figures of our day."

B103 M.B.P. *Bulletin of the East Midwood Jewish Center*,
November 1, 1957, p. 3.

"I disagree with [reviewers who] generally have rated *The
Assistant* an excellent modern literary achievement. . . . It is
startling fiction which reads easily, which is exciting and
different. Yet as for plausibility . . . I cannot ascribe to it the
realism that the author hopes to attain for us."

B104 Michelfelder, William. "*A Brooklyn Grocer Rich in
Compassion*," New York *World Telegram and Sun*,
May 2, 1957, p.27.

"Novelist Malamud is an eloquent apologist for the dignity of
poverty. . . . No man can pray on an empty stomach . . . but
Mr. Malamud is not so much concerned with that hoary cliché
as he is with human courage that can do without prayer and
funds. . . . In his novel [unlike those of James T. Farrell and
Nelson Algren] the poor have a glow. . . . They are . . .
uncommon individuals who draw surprising strength from
their . . . hopeless struggle. . . . These people emerge unscathed
as fine human beings."

B105 Poore, Charles. New York *Times*, May 9, 1957, p. 29.

". . . Here is Mr. Malamud with a haunting, probing
nocturne of unfulfilled lives in New York's metropolitan
wasteland. . . . One lives the lives of the people in *The
Assistant* as one reads the book."

B106 Ribalow, Harold U. "A Genuine Jewish Novel,"
Congress Weekly, May 13, 1957, p.16.

"Malamud's novel will be read . . . for many years to come. . . .
We are in the presence of a brilliant stylist, a moralist, a
novelist who looks deep into the heart. . . . Malamud's people,
once accepted, win our sympathy; yet they are not easy to
fathom. . . . The . . . brevity of the tale adds to its
impressiveness."

B107 Rogers, W. G. "Bravo, Malamud," New York *Post*,
April 28, 1957, p. M-11.

"I can't whoop it up enough for this novel and this novelist.
Malamud is wonderfully the master of a major talent, and a
most exciting one, too, with many facets; he knows the way to
the funny bone as well as to the heart; every word
spoken by his incredibly real people rings with the bottom
truth; no neighborhood secret . . . escapes his loving and
implacable probe; he plots like a whiz; and he is a moralist."

B108 Roth, H. L. *Library Journal*, LXXII
(April 15, 1967), 1067.

"Well written, but with scenes of brutality, this is not to be
recommended to the reader who wants light gay fiction; it is for
the public library with a cosmopolitan clientele."

B109 Sullivan, Richard. Chicago *Sunday Tribune*, May 19,
1957, "Books Today," 7.

"In the lives of the persons moving through this novel there is
nothing tragic, or heroic or even impressively dramatic. Yet
every person presented is made remarkably real."

B110 Swados, Harvey. "The Emergence of An Artist:
Bernard Malamud," *Western Review*, XXVI
(Winter 1958), 148-151.

With the entrance of Frankie Alpine into the novel, "we move
with Bernard Malamud into a new dimension, and we are
lifted into a new realm of vision. . . . Now we begin to see that
this is no mere breastbeating tale of poor Jews, although
it is always that too. It is a saga of alienation and frustration, of

man's yearning for brotherhood and his fear of
communion. . . . *The Assistant* is one novel in a thousand and . . .
Malamud is one writer in a thousand. . . . [The novel provides]
the opportunity for purgation and consequently . . . a deeper
insight into the conditions of [the readers'] own lives."

B111 *Time*, LXIX (April 29, 1957), 100.

"In his second book, [Malamud] goes deeper [than in
The Natural] into human nature, and the result is an even
more impressive novel to delight admirers in the growing
Malamud salon."

B112 Wagner, Charles A. New York *Mirror*, June 23, 1957, p. 7.

"This is . . . told with such lean, clean felicity that it holds you
by sheer reality. The grocer's daughter marries the Gentile
assistant and the integration is completed in other ways too, but,
like Daniel Fuchs of old, Malamud has a genius for
authentic dialogue you can't afford to miss."

The Magic Barrel

B113 Bahr, Jerome. "A Collection of Thirteen Fine Stories,"
Baltimore *Sun*, May 18, 1958, p. 21.

"Malamud is at home [both in stories of] Jewish tenement folk
in New York and middle-class American intellectuals visiting
in Italy. The former are handled in classic folk-tale style, the
latter satirically. . . . [but] there is depth and tenderness
[in the former] that make the other stories seem almost
superficial in comparison. . . . All of these stories are written
simply and well, but it is at those moments when Malamud
places his folk ethic in opposition to materialistic strivings that
he attains his greatest depth and strength."

B114 Blackman, R. C. *Christian Science Monitor*,
May 15, 1958, p. 11.

" . . . a collection of short stories unified by a tone of resigned
and humorous wisdom and an unsentimental central

compassion. . . . *The Magic Barrel* . . . has the simplicity of expression that is a product of good writing and good feeling, and that is so conspicuously missing from many contemporary best-sellers in fiction."

B115 Bryden, Ronald. *Spectator*, June 30, 1960, p. 810.

"*The Magic Barrel* [possesses] unusual grace and spareness with which [it works] the slightly hackneyed field of New York Jewish humor. . . . but Mr. Malamud has a trick of leading his simple O. Henry anecdotes to suddenly complex, reverberant endings."

B116 "A Correct Compassion," *The Times* (London) *Literary Supplement*, April 1, 1960, p. 205.

"Collected stories . . . reveal variety within homogeneity, a world 'cornered' . . . . subtleties, in which the paradox of guilt and happiness, the irony of good intentions and all human struggles against suffering, are suggested sometimes by a single poetic image, a juxtaposition of gross trivialities with romantic and mystical thought."

B117 Foff, Arthur. *Northwest Review*, I (Fall-Winter 1958), 63-67.

"The Jew is a typical figure in *The Magic Barrel* not because Malamud is exclusively interested in a given religion or race, but because the Jew is for him, as for all of us, a perduring symbol of him who would preserve the spirit despite his own absolute loneliness and defeat. . . . [Malamud insists] on the universality of such isolation."

B118 Jacobson, Dan. "Magic and Morality," *Commentary*, XXIV (October 1958), 359-361.

"Great gifts are displayed in the stories . . . [but] . . . his work is *not* marginal or dreamlike. . . . and the force and logic of his stories tends to fail. . . . His strengths are of the most important kind."

B119 Klein, Marcus. "Imps from Bottles, Etc." *Hudson Review*, XII (Winter 1958-1959), 624-625.

> Malamud . . . "knows what he knows—not even Jewish life, really, but the imperatives of suffering and pity as they happen to be postulated for him by Jewish life. . . . His people exist not in society but in romance. . . . It is still his intimate and fabulous image of grace that makes him the exciting writer he is."

B120 "Old Men of the Sea," *Time*, LXXI (May 12, 1958), 104.

> "Malamud is primarily a fantasist who starts out with people as sweaty and real as subway rush-hour passengers, but soon has them clothed in white and silver and singing hosannahs. . . . At his best he is as funny and earthy as . . . Sholom Aleichem. . . . But in his transfigured view of the world he may be even closer to Francois Mauriac, the Catholic moralist."

B121 Peden, William. "Dogged by a Sense of Injustice and Grief," New York *Times Book Review*, May 11, 1958, p. 5.

> "[An] atavistic identification with grief permeates all these moving stories . . . [yet] they bubble with life."

B122 Poore, Charles. The New York *Times*, May 10, 1958, p. 19.

> "The stories in *The Magic Barrel* do not dwell on [the spread of barbarism] at any length, but they evade it in a phrase, a descriptive passage, a memory of irremediable sorrow."

B123 Popkin, Henry. "Jewish Stories," *Kenyon Review*, XX (Autumn 1958), 637-641.

> "Malamud loves his Jews; in fact, he loves humanity, compassion, and all the virtues. . . . He is saved [from sentimentality] . . . by a certain irreducible sourness in most of his characters and by the intransigence of the circumstances he has created."

B124 Rugoff, Milton. "Making Everyday Life Glow," New York *Herald Tribune Sunday Book Review*, May 25, 1958, p. 3.

" . . . Like the so-called Magic Realist in painting—he is master of an alchemy whereby the grossest reality is converted to the most imaginative uses. He transcribes everyday life and yet the result glows with lights never seen on land or sea. . . . In his hands, the line between the cruel and the kind, the holy and profane, the grotesque and the beautiful is redrawn in a dozen inspired ways."

B125 Schickel, Richard. "Decline of the Short Story," *The Progressive*, XXII (September 1958), 50-51.

"There is a sentimentality to these tales, as well as a condescending cuteness which mars them seriously. . . . In short, they are emotional clichés."

B126 Sullivan, Richard. Chicago *Sunday Tribune*, May 18, 1958, "Books Today," p. 3.

"This is the kind of book that calls for not only admiration but gratitude; for it is a rare pleasure to read work so purely and justly written. . . . The charm lies in the profound concern shown in every story for people, for human existence itself, for what might even be called the holiness of life."

B127 Swados, Harvey. "Barrelful of Charm," New York *Post*, May 10, 1958, p. 10.

"Vision is what informs the stories of Malamud. . . . It can now be seen that [he] is our finest natural-born story-teller since Sherwood Anderson. . . . Malamud's secret . . . lies in his love and compassion for his fellow humans. That, and the capacity he shares with the finest artists for understanding that what is most profoundly and remarkably human in us all is to be found as readily—if not more readily—in the humblest of men as in the aristocratic."

B128 Tucker, Martin. "A Pluralistic Place," *Venture*, III (1959), 69-73.

"All through Malamud's stories runs this persistent theme: man is his brother's keeper because it is only in 'keeping' one's brother that one really becomes a man. Thus all of Malamud's heroes mature in the same way: they learn to see . . . an inimical viewpoint . . . and then embrace it in an overt or implicit act of love."

B129 Waterhouse, Keith. "New Short Stories," *New Statesman*, LIX (May 14, 1960), 725-726.

"One reason why I salute Mr. Malamud is that in *The Magic Barrel* he keeps right off the hokum-schmokum, I should-drop-dead folksy kind of Jewish story for which, I am sure, we would have been . . . grateful. . . . The man has style."

B130 Weales, Gerald. "The Sharing of Misery," *The New Leader*, XLI (September 1, 1958), 24-25.

"Although the stories in *The Magic Barrel* differ in quality, none of them fails to place the reader with the protagonist in space, time and pain. . . . In trying to define the ways in which Malamud is Jewish I have become involved in the recognition of agony, the love that is the sharing of pain, the fear that is the rejection of pity and the wonder that is the strengthening of men. The idiom is Jewish; the central concern is human."

B131 Whitbread, Jane. *Good Housekeeping*, CL (March 1960), 55.

"Bernard Malamud's bare prose, reminiscent of the language of Biblical parables, recounts with monotonous insistence the grim facts of loveless life. . . . In short doses he is interesting, but long exposure . . . is not for me."

A New Life

B132 Adams, Phoebe. "The Burdens of the Past," *Atlantic*,
CCVIII (November 1961), 104-105.

"[*A New Life*] . . . is a very well-written novel which ultimately
disappoints the reader by being more conventional in subject
and attitude than Mr. Malamud's previous books. . . . Mr.
Malamud has not added anything notable to the established
pictures of spiritual progress, academic gutter fighting or
provincial stagnation . . ."

B133 Berman, R. S. "Totems of Liberalism," *Modern Age*,
VI (Spring 1962), 212.

"[Levin, the hero] believes in non-conformity without ever
discovering that the idea is inapplicable when divorced from its
religious origins and ineffectual when made to serve an end
in itself. The book is full of small allegiances to great ideas, yet
it is shamefully barren of their elucidation."

B134 Bowen, Robert O. *National Review*, XI (December 2,
1961), 383.

"Throughout Malamud's prose, both *A New Life* and in his
earlier novels, one incident after another debases
idealizations articulated through the flesh. . . . the book insists
that all the fleshly world . . . is somewhat raunchy. . . .
[It] gives a clear report of normal state university life . . .
departmental espionage, blackmail, subordination, and assorted
shenanigans."

B135 Daniels, Sally. "Flights and Evasions," *Minnesota
Review*, II (Summer 1962), 551-554.

". . . Malamud is the first American I know of able to write
about the college community and more or less transcend . . .
the 'academic novel.' " The novel does not "confirm his
place as one of our important novelists" because despite "a
rich welter of the rendered detail of life, [it lacks] the sense of
fully realized characters."

B136 DeMott, Benjamin. *Hudson Review*, XIV (Winter 1961-1962) 628-629.

> "The stuff of *A New Life* is only a tenth as pliant as the black unknown metropolis but the book establishes that even the most commonplace stuff can be talked into meaning—if the voice that speaks is complicated enough, if it can sound (all at once) passionate and objective, idealistic and cynical, hopeless and hopeful, exalted and ruined. . . . [It affirms] that there still is almost nothing that is *absolutely* impossible for art."

B137 Elman, Richard M. "Malamud on Campus," *Commonweal*, LXXV (October 27, 1961), 114-115.

> *A New Life* "fails to be convincing." Its strengths—accurate description of landscape—do not compensate for its dreariness.

B138 Goodheart, Eugene. "Fantasy and Reality," *Midstream*, VII (Autumn 1961), 102-105.

> "It is as if the novelist has to work *against* reality, to perform through fantasy, pastoral dream and mythic re-creation of the past the acts of faith that make the celebration of life still possible . . . but when the actual world comes to us again, the dream becomes a kind of irony in our lives."

B139 Halley, Anne. "The Good Life in Recent Fiction," *Massachusetts Review*, III (Autumn 1961), 190-196.

> "Levin manages to be both ridiculous and heroic. . . . He is weak . . . yet fated to act with a sense of mission; from the first he exists outside the glibly organized cause-and-effect context in which character is too often limited and action too often explained by diluted psychiatric concepts."

B140 Hartt, J. N. "The Return of Moral Passion," *Yale Review*, LI (Winter 1962), 300.

> "I do not think that . . . ambiguity is a virtue in a novel. . . . While Malamud seems to want the reader to admire the . . .

stirrings of courage and wisdom in his hero . . . he can't pass up
the joke—the situations in which Levin is a clown without
grace of wit."

B141 Hicks, Granville. *Saturday Review*, XLIV (October 7,
1961), 20.

"Malamud is one of the notable characters of contemporary
American literature. . . . In *A New Life* he has taken most
unpromising materials and, by virtue of insight, technical
mastery, and a kind of heroic quality in himself, has made out
of them an exciting and memorable novel!"

B142 Hollander, John. *Partisan Review*, XXIX (Winter
1962), 137-139.

". . . Its new version of an old American pastoral encounter
redeems it from the provinces of any smaller genre. It is a
unique kind of book, and for its author's future work, it
promises excellent results."

B143 Hyman, Stanley Edgar. "A New Life for a Good Man,"
New Leader, XLIV (October 2, 1961), 24-25.
". . . . *A New Life* is a new novel of consistent excellence . . .
a fable of redemption or rebirth. . . . The action of the
novel is Levin's development into a kind of saint. . . . If
Malamud continues to be able to find modern plots to embody
his powerful redemptive themes, I know no limits to what
he can accomplish." Reprinted in B13 and B14.

B144 Jebb, Julian. "As Good as the Blurbs Say," *Time and
Tide*, XLIII (March 29, 1962), 40.

"The best part of this deeply depressing novel is the opening
scenes in which Levin . . . is established (most concretely)
as a symbol of the loneliness which accrues to the reformed . . .
Malamud's seriousness and intelligence are always apparent . . .
what is missing . . . is an unambiguously realized central
character."

B145 Kermode, Frank. "Bernard Malamud," *New Statesman*, LXIII (March 30, 1962), 452-453.

Malamud's work is "a ghetto dream colored by a New World environment." In *A New Life*, he has the problem of the "sentimentality of old-world Jewishness."

B146 Malcolm, Donald. *New Yorker*, XXXVI (January 28, 1967), 105.

"[Malamud] has collected a staggering amount of information on every deplorable aspect of the academic life. . . . Levin adds to the . . . bifurcation of the novel [because of] his reluctance to engage in controversy which produces a serious disconnection in the novel."

B147 Maloff, Saul. "Between the Real and the Absurd," *Nation*, CXCIII (November 18, 1961), 407.

"If we say that Malamud's world is like no other, it is because the world he creates occupies the air exactly between the real and the absurd, where only saints and lunatics are, and where the right gesture . . . can save one's life, or some other. [This novel presents] some of the best landscape and nature writing . . . some of the most sensitive and joyous writing about women and sexual love . . . and certainly the deftest, most delicious satire of the cynicism and stupidity of the academy."

B148 Manning, Olivia. "Under the Influence," *Spectator*, March 30, 1962, p. 421.

"*A New Life* has sporadic brilliance, but as a successor to *The Assistant* it is a disappointment. . . . The nullity of its hero, Levin, is defeating its creator."

B149 Oboler, Eli. *Library Journal*, LXXXVII (October 1, 1961), 3302.

". . . Written with crystal clear style . . . but with plot and characterization not as individual as in his early works. . . . comes close [to being] entirely dull and obvious . . ."

B150 "Passions and Dilemmas," *Newsweek*, LVIII (October 9, 1961), 105.

"Malamud is beginning to be recognized as one of the finest living American fiction writers. . . . His means are utterly traditional (stemming from Flaubert) . . . [and] one of his main strengths is the gradual growth and shifting of human passions and dilemmas, the long flux of emotions. . . .[the novel ends as] that rare fictional achievement, true tragi-farce."

B151 Pickrel, Paul. *Harper's*, CCXXIII (November 1961), 120.

"*A New Life* is something of a disappointment, not only because of Malamud's generous endowment as a writer but also because in this book he starts with what seems like a fine subject for a novel and essentially wastes its opportunities."

B152 Price, R. G. G. *Punch*, CCXLII (May 9, 1961), 733.

". . . how refreshing to find a character who is not the same all the time. . . . The novel has learnt how to make people develop but hardly begun to . . . represent mood."

B153 Rubin, Louis D. Jr. "Six Novels and S. Levin," *Sewanee Review*, LXX (Summer 1962) 504.

Malamud "has created a protagonist who seems fully human, who cannot be lightly satirized or made ridiculous, who can take advantage of the full range of his intelligence and perceptions, who emerges from his ordeal as a compromised but nonetheless an honest man. He is a very strange phenomenon in contemporary fiction; he is a hero."

B154 Solotaroff, Theodore. "Bernard Malamud's Fiction: the Old Life and the New," *Commentary*, XXXIII (March 1962), 197-204.

The novel continues Malamud's concerns with "the fact that man is confronted less with the world than with himself. . . . In illustrating the uncertainties of our time, Malamud does not quite get beyond the old life."

B155 Stevenson, David L. "The Strange Destiny of S. Levin," New York *Times Book Review*, October 8, 1961, p. 1.

> "The special qualities of Bernard Malamud's fiction which set it apart as serious art and yet keep it in a minor key, are its evocation of genuine pity ... its scrupulous and deft playing of an ironic attitude against this pity, and its insistently moral structuring of event. . . . [This novel] will have a much wider appeal than his earlier books. . . . yet I do not find this as compelling ... as *The Assistant*, perhaps because of its mixed intentions."

B156 *Virginia Quarterly Review*, XXXVIII (Winter 1962).

> ". . . Mr. Malamud follows the short and unhappy career of a Bloomlike central figure ... [who] ultimately meets his doom. . . . The book is certain to bring wry smiles from his readers in the groves of academe."

B157 Voss, Arthur. *Books Abroad*, XXXV (Winter 1962), 79.

> "There is some effective satire of academic manners and mores ... [but] ... what gives the novel its power is the pervasive irony associated with its hero whose efforts to give of his best and to maintain his integrity ... seem doomed ... to turn out badly."

B158 West, Jessamyn. New York *Herald Tribune Book Review*, October 8, 1961, p. 4.

> "[Malamud's] theme ... remains what was in his much-praised novel, *The Assistant*, the assimilation of a man by those to whom he comes in the first instance as an outsider; an assimilation which the outsider at first resists, then works for with all his heart. And the heart is the organ which does the work ... [Levin's] awakening to nature is as much a part of his new life as his awakening to love, and Malamud writes of it with the conviction of a man telling a story at first hand."

B159 "The Wild Man from the East," *Time*, LXXVIII (October 6, 1961), 96.

"*A New Life* is written primarily in realistic terms, and in these terms it often fails. . . . But Malamud remains . . . expert . . . in his persuasive alternations of farce and sadness, the tender Chekovian qualities that have marked all his work."

Idiots First

B160 Alter, Robert. "Out of the Trap," *Midstream*, IX (December 1963), 88.

"One major aspect of Malamud's sensibility that has redeemed his stories of ensnarement from being merely oppressive is the compassion he has shown, and often managed to make felt, for his suffering protagonists."

B161 Dupee, F. W. "The Power of Positive Sex," *Partisan Review*, XXXI, (Summer 1964), 425-430.

"Malamud's ability to persuade us of the reality of his characters—their emotions, deeds, words, surroundings— remains astonishing. . . . Malamud can be aligned with such writers as J. F. Powers rather than with . . . Jewish- American writers of today, to whom he is generally compared." Reprinted in B5.

B162 Hassan, Ihab. New York *Times Book Review*, October 13, 1963, p. 5.

Bernard Malamud's "response to the human condition is deep; it is revealed with breathtaking skill. . . . The voice of conscience is audible in the beat of words, in the crackle of metaphor . . . it is everywhere in Malamud's work."

B163 ———. Letter on his review of *Idiots First*, New York *Times Book Review*, October 27, 1963, p. 65.

Hassan protests the omission of the final paragraph from his review. In the paragraph he suggests that tactful and controlled response to outrage may not be enough . . . "the great winged genius of our time may . . . welcome the end of things and herald a second coming of man."

B164 Igoe, William J. Chicago *Tribune*, November 17, 1963, p. 8.

"Pain he [Malamud] finds funny; he satirizes agony."

B165 Leibowitz, Herbert. "Malamud and the Anthropomorphic Business," *New Republic*, CXLIX (December 21, 1963), 21-23.

"Malamud is a sort of waggish minstrel of misery. He is a homilist whose stock of canny folk proverbs contains the distilled wisdom of the politics of survival. . . . Like . . . Aeschylus . . . Malamud explores the dialectic of law and love."

B166 Levine, Norman. "Stockpot," *Spectator*, June 12, 1964, 802-803.

"There is a makeshift look about this volume of short stories; from the evidence of the stories . . . I'd say that Mr. Malamud's talent is much better displayed in his novels."

B167 Malin, Irving. *Reconstructionist*, XXIX (November 29, 1963), 25-28.

The stories "reinterpret the traditional moments of exile, suffering, and family life in striking ways."

B168 Meixner, John. *Sewanee Review*, LXXII (Summer 1964), 540-542.

". . . Malamud is at present engaged in searching for a subject . . . beyond that of New York Jewish life, which has been at his creative center . . . [but] . . . as yet is not truly at home in a less parochial world. He still has his best successes in the old Jewish milieu."

B169 Mitgang, Herbert. New York *Times*, October 14, 1963, p. 27.

Malamud's short stories are "blood brothers to Chagall's paintings . . . with . . . tragic vision and . . . ebullient joy . . ."

B170 *Newsweek*, LXIII (October 7, 1963), 112.

"The proper use of fantasy—as a means not of escaping reality but of heightening it—is a rarity, but Malamud never falters."

B171 Oberbeck, S. K. "The Measured Tread of Catastrophe," St. Louis *Post-Dispatch*, September 22, 1964, p. 2-B.

"His tone of voice . . . shuffles between humorous and tragic, but his deeper tone never changes: there is always the ring of impending tragedy."

B172 Perlberg, Mark. "Malamud has Moral Mettle," Detroit *Free Press*, October 20, 1963, Section B, p. 5.

"What is . . . impressive about Malamud is his moral force. It is this . . . that makes him one of the two or three most important writers in the country today."

B173 Pickrel, Paul. "Selected Shorts," *Harper's*, CCXXVII (November 1963), 130, 132.

Malamud has the "ability to write many different *kinds* of story."

B174 Raphael, Frederic. "Stealth and the Outer Life," London *Sunday Times*, May 31, 1964, p. 39.

"What counts is the specific portraiture, the command of mood and atmosphere, the sense of fantasy which never loses its pertinence to lived life."

B175 Ribalow, Harold U. "*Idiots First* Reviewed," *Congress Bi-Weekly*, November, 1963, p. 18, 19.

"His art sometimes falters. When it succeeds, he is incomparable."

B176 Rogers, W. G. "Stories of Lonely People Prove a Theory," New York *World-Telegram and Sun*, October 9, 1963, p. 56.

". . . Malamud tells us today as he has before . . . Nobody is

common or drab; everyone has hopes; for everyone they are
fulfilled or dashed."

B177 Sale, Roger, *Hudson Review*, XVI (Winter
1963-1964), 607.

"Malamud's trademark, the confusions of the lost, only works
when the characters are not flatly understood. . . . as yet
Malamud still has one métier of which he is the master."

B178 Solotaroff, Theodore. "Showing Us 'What It Means
Human,' " *Book Week*, October 13, 1963, p. 5.

In *Idiots First*, one sees "an opening up and outwards of
Malamud himself, his new taking of stock and initiative."

B179 Staley, Thomas F. "The Core of Life," Pittsburgh *Press*,
November 10, 1963, Section V, p. 11.

". . . His talent grows richer . . . and this collection marks
another landmark in Malamud's career."

B180 Taubman, Robert. "People of the Law," *New
Statesman*, LXVI (June 5, 1964), 883.

"So far as we deserve or are likely to get one, Bernard
Malamud's stories might be part of a Divine Comedy of our
time. . . . I doubt if unaccommodated man has had a fairer
or a better defense by any other modern novelist."

B181 Wagner, Mary H. *America*, CIX (October 26, 1963),
490.

". . . stories of Malamud—sometimes crazy, often vulgar, but
always drawn with vigor, beautifully paced, and proceeding
by inversion to the realities of life."

B182 Wheildon, Leonard. Boston *Herald*, October 20, 1963,
Section 4, p. 3.

The stories . . . "portray the infinite complexity of human
character, comedy in tragedy, tragedy in comedy, and always the
shocking truth."

The Fixer

B183 Alexander, James L. "Sordid Testimony of Man's Inhumanity to Man," Pittsburgh *Post-Gazette*, September 24, 1966, p. 19.

". . . You must read that each man has choices which he must make, and that there is good in each man."

B184 Alter, Robert. "Malamud as Jewish Writer," *Commentary*, XLII (September 1966), 71-76.

"*The Fixer* shares with Bernard Malamud's earlier fiction the theme that moral involvement is necessary . . . once again Malamud makes successful symbolic use of the Jew as Everyman. . . . Malamud is to the best of my knowledge the first important American writer to shape out of his early experiences in the immigrant milieu a whole distinctive style of imagination and, to a lesser degree, a distinctive technique of fiction as well. . . . 'One thing I've learned . . . there's no such thing as an unpolitical man, especially a Jew,' [a statement of Bok in *The Fixer*]. . . . nicely states the relationship between the particular and the universal in this novel and in Malamud's work as a whole."

B185 Balliett, Whitney. "Rub-a-Dub-Dub," *New Yorker*, XLII (December 10, 1966), 234-235.

"Human misery does not catalog well. . . . The reader is finally repelled."

B186 Barkham, John "The Fixer—an Ordinary Man," San Francisco *Examiner and Chronicle*, October 23, 1966, pp. 37-38.

The article quotes Malamud as saying, "My aim was to show how [Yakov] could stand up under the terrible strains to which he was subjected."

B187 ———. "The Undefeated," *Review of the Latest New Books*, September 3, 1966, p. 4.

The Fixer is . . . "a study in courage . . . which is . . . a *real* novel . . . which depends for its effect on the traditional virtues of form, structure, imagination, and style."

B188 Bellman, Samuel I. Los Angeles *Times*, August 21, 1966, "Calender" Section, p. 16.

In this novel, Malamud goes "backward and downward" . . . in his career. He has written a "non-novel."

B189 Bresler, Riva T. *Library Journal*, XCI (October 15, 1966), p. 3470.

"Superb in its meticulous analysis. . . . reminiscent of *The Plague* . . . but . . . Harrowing and perhaps over-detailed."

B190 Burgess, Anthony. "Blood in the Matzos," *Spectator*, April 14, 1967, pp. 424-425.

"It is . . . stupid to be disappointed that Malamud has not given us what he has already given us so well—the working of the spirit in an exactly rendered contemporary Jewish-American scene. . . . The conjuration of a dead era and city is brilliant. . . . [but] . . . *The Fixer*, one feels, is a pastiche of a writer who never existed but, in order to fill a historical gap, ought to have existed."

B191 Cevasco, George. *The Sign*, December, 1966, p. 19.

Malamud is quoted as saying, "I write about Jews because Jews are absolutely the very stuff of drama."

B192 Cook, Don L. "Malamud's Scapegoat Novel: Its Factual Basis," Louisville *Courier-Journal*, September 25, 1966, Section D., p. 5.

"It is compelling and convincing because [Malamud] has drawn [Yakov] for us in warm, not in cold blood."

B193 Davis, Robert Gorham. "Invaded Selves," *Hudson Review*, XIX (Winter 1966-1967), 659-668.

Yakov's views . . . sympathetic though they may be to us . . . seem to have "flowed from Malamud's mind" rather than from Yakov.

B194 Degnan, James P. "The Ordeal of Yakov Bok," *The Critic*, xxv (October 1966), 102-104.

The Fixer is that rarity . . . "a straightforward 'philosophical' novel and a realistic novel of ideas that is artistically successful."

B195 Elliott, George P. "Yakov's Ordeal," New York *Times Book Review*, September 4, 1966, pp. 1, 25-26.

"Maybe the political and metaphysical are two aspects of his one supreme story. In any case, at the end of *The Fixer* he let the two modes get in each other's way."

B196 Ehrmann, Herbert B. Boston *Herald*, September 18, 1966, "Show Guide," p. 21.

". . . In more than three thousand years, we have not yet reached the foot of Mount Sinai. Of this, Malamud's story is a disturbing reminder."

B197 Elkin, Stanley. *Massachusetts Review*, ix (Spring, 1967) 388-392.

"*The Fixer* is immensely moving but . . . this is . . . its supreme achievement and part of its downfall."

B198 Fanger, Donald. "*The Fixer* in Another Country," *The Nation*, cciii (October 17, 1966), pp. 389-390.

In *The Fixer* Malamud has . . . "staked a claim in the territory of Dostoevski and Tolstoy (not to mention Kafka.)"

B199 Fremont-Smith, Eliot. "Yakov's Choice," New York *Times*, August 29, 1966, p. 27.

". . . One of the year's richest novels, a literary event in any season; one wishes that it functioned not almost perfectly, but perfectly."

B200 Friedberg, Maurice. "History and Imagination — Two Views of the Beiliss Case," *Midstream*, XII (November 1966), 71-76.

"Mr. Malamud's distillation of history into a product of artistic imagination demonstrates the firm hand of a skilled craftsman."

B201 Friend, James. "Malamud's Heroic Handyman a Symbol of Universal Woe," Chicago *Daily News*, September 10, 1966, "Panorama" Section, p. 7.

". . . Writers like Malamud continue to offer us the light of choice within the shadows of our present day challenges."

B202 Fuller, Edmund. "Malamud's Novel Aims High but Falls Short," *Wall Street Journal*, September 9, 1966, p. 12.

The novel has "moments of beauty, power, and dignity . . . but . . . it is flawed."

B203 Geltman, Max. "Irrational Streams of Blood," *National Review*, XVIII, November 1, 1966, pp. 1117-1119.

"In his attempt to heighten the drama . . . Bernard Malamud has indicated to us the secular striving for an out from God and moral sanction in order to play the devil with history."

B204 German, Bob. Houston *Post*, September 4, 1966, p. 10.

This is the book "the Russians couldn't write but should have."

B205 Greene, A. C. "A Book with a Backbone," Dallas *Times-Herald*, September 4, 1966, p. E-7.

"*The Fixer* is a novel of good and evil, clearly drawn, but primarily, it is a novel of human importance."

B206 Greenfield, Josh. *Book Week*, September 11, 1966, p. 1.

"*The Fixer* contains many moments that are monuments to compassionate artistry."

B207 Handy, William J. "Malamud's *The Fixer*: Another Look," *Northwest Review*, IX (Spring 1967), 74-82.

> Earlier review (Robert Scholes's) in *Northwest Review* did not do justice to the theme of *The Fixer*, which is "freedom of self allows man to join the universe."

B208 Hardwick, Elizabeth, *Vogue*, CXLVIII (September 1, 1966), 208.

> "Historical reality combined with fictional skill and beauty of a high order make . . . a novel of startling importance."

B209 Hicks, Granville. *Saturday Review*, XLIX (September 10, 1966), 37-38.

> "One of the finest novels of the postwar period . . . [has] the universal meanings of legend."

B210 Hogan, William. "Malamud's Crime and Punishment," San Francisco *Chronicle*, September 7, 1966, p. 39.

> "Basically, *The Fixer*, a powerful novel . . . is a study of the undefeated."

B211 Halliday, Barbara. "A Prisoner of the Czar: Jakov Bok's Ritual Torture," Detroit *Free Press*, September 11, 1966, Section B, p. 5.

> The story of the oppressed in every society is a powerful theme but . . . "torture beyond a certain point arouses revulsion rather than compassion."

B212 Jackson, Katherine Gauss. *Harper's*, CCXXXIII (October 1966), 127.

> "The [reader's] mind reels with pride in [Yakov's] human achievement and one's identification with Yakov is complete."

B213 Jacobson, Dan. "The Old Country," *Partisan Review*, XXXIV (Spring 1967), 307-309.

> "A strikingly uneven book. . . . Imparts a sense of foreboding

which expresses its moral and historical burden but . . . is . . . clumsy in technique and uncertain in tone."

B214 Jaffe, Dan. Kansas City *Star*, September 11, 1966, p. 7-E.

A magnificent literary event, comparable with *Crime and Punishment*, this novel is . . . "for the living and for the not yet born. . . . As long as man knows grief, injustice, pain, courage, and doubt this book will be contemporary."

B215 Kennedy, William. "The Frightening Beiliss Case in Fictional Scholarly Perspective," *National Observer*, September 5, 1966, p. 19.

"Mr. Malamud's story stands . . . as a rare and excellent creation of a man totally alone."

B216 Killinger, John. *Christian Herald*, March 1967, p. 50.

It "illumines the specifically human problems [involved in] 'the experience of God's absence.' "

B217 King, Francis. "Wrenched from Obscurity," London *Sunday Telegraph*, April 9, 1967, p. 9.

"A magnificent, if profoundly depressing novel . . . . suggests Dostoevski. . . . Its fault is that the author provides his own trite programme notes . . . but . . . certainly no better novel has appeared for several months."

B218 *Kirkus Bulletin*, xxxiv (July 1, 1966), 102.

The Fixer has ". . . exposed humanity. . . . It is a work of commanding power."

B219 Kitching, Jessie. *Publishers' Weekly*, June 27, 1966, p. 96.

Bok's "persecution is a crystallization of the special cruelty of man to man in modern times."

B220 Lockerbie, D. Bruce. *Eternity*, February 1967, p. 56.

"The Fixer is not . . . merely another Semitic tract. . . . To a

Christian this novel . . . disturbs because one wants to cry
out, 'But those aren't *real* Christians!' "

B221 Ludlow, Francis. *Book Buyer's Almanac*, September
1966, p. 121.

"It's a haunting novel that deserves to be read again and again.
. . . Editor's choice of the month."

B222 Lynch, William S. Providence *Sunday Journal*,
September 11, 1966, p. H-9.

"No one deserves the word [compassionate] more than
Bernard Malamud. . . . It truly must be called great!"

B223 Maddocks, Melvin. "Malamud's Heroic Handyman,"
Christian Science Monitor, September 8, 1966, p. 13.

"He has produced a *bona fide* hero. . . . It could . . . make
available to the American novel a toughened new set of
human possibilities. . . . These pages are as thick and pungent
as a slice of black bread."

B224 Marcus, Mordecai. "The Unsuccessful Malamud,"
Prairie Schooner, XLI (Spring 1967), 88-89.

". . . The failure of sensibility in *The Fixer* seems to stem from
the interaction of recalcitrant material and inept technique."

B225 Mathewson, Joseph. *Harper's Bazaar*, XCIX
(November 1966), 116.

"*The Fixer* . . . may deserve to be classed with Kafka's *The
Trial*. . . . [Its] pages are more immediate in . . . impact . . .
than *The Trial*."

B226 P. S. Detroit *Jewish News*, September 9, 1966, p. 36.

". . . A great novel and a superb social document."

B227 Pasley, Virginia. "Review of *The Fixer*," *Newsday*,
September 3, 1966.

"... The theme of the book is more specifically Jewish than any
of Malamud's novels.... But it is ... more universal in that
it deals with ... the falsely accused."

B228 Petersen, Betsy. "Idea of Freedom Won Through
Suffering," New Orleans *Times-Picayune*, November 6,
1966, Section III, p. 16.

"This is ... one of the greatest novels of any season. ... It is
also in a sense, one of the worst. It is an agonizing, though
extraordinary experience. ... which the reader must share with
the hero. How it hurts!"

B229 Peterson, Virgilia. *The Reporter*, XXXV (October 20,
1966), 57.

"*The Fixer* as a study of man against fate, has literary distinction
... but ... fact has the edge ... over ... even the most loftily
conceived fictional version."

B230 Petrakis, Harry Mark. "One Man's Battle Against
Injustice," Chicago *Tribune Books Today*, September 11,
1966, p. 1.

"In the end the little fixer becomes a blazing figure wearing
the raiment of tragedy. ... Illuminated by his suffering
and torment [he] becomes a deep and pathetic symbol ..."

B231 Prescott, Peter S. *Women's Wear Daily*, August 26,
1966, p. 44.

"*The Fixer* asks a unique question: 'When a man is called upon
to account for himself in terms of a perversion of a birthright
that has always embarrassed him, what is he to say, and more
important, what is he to do?' "

B232 Pritchett, V. S. "A Pariah," New York *Review of Books*, September 22, 1966, pp. 8-9. (Illustrated by caricature of Bernard Malamud by David Levine.)

"Malamud gets into Bok's mind by a kind of passive cunning very much a feature of this novelist's writing. . . . The whole fable is unexpected, inventive, and compelling."

B233 Quigley, Martin. "Yakov, Fixer of Everything but the Heart," St. Louis *Globe-Democrat*, September 17, 1966, p. 4-F.

"A hero of truth rises in this inspiring and majestic story of the struggle of naked innocence against the power of tyrants."

B234 Ratner, Marc. "The Humanism of Malamud's *The Fixer*," *Critique*, IX (1967), 81-84.

"The nature of human suffering, as Malamud expresses it in *The Fixer*, is that nothing is so individual and universal in a man's experience as pain. Malamud's hero moves from being 'fixed' by circumstances and events to being the 'fixer.' He begins with the 'rock of atheism' pain, and ends by affirming his faith in an act of moral engagement."

B235 Richler, Mordecai. "Write, Boycheck, Write," *New Statesman*, LXXII (April 7, 1967), 473-474.

"It is a worthy novel but in the end . . . it is curiously without an inner life, a will of its own. . . . It is forced in the humanist's greenhouse . . ."

B236 Rosenthal, Raymond. "A Christian Problem," *New Leader*, XLIX (September 12, 1966), 18-19.

"The dark residue that remains [of anti-Semitism] after all the explanations are given—this is his subject."

B237 Samuels, Charles Thomas. "The Career of Bernard Malamud," *New Republic*, CLV (September 10, 1966), 19.

"It is a small but real defeat for us all that Malamud (a precious

national heritage) has traded his dark place so lighted by
crazy sparks for a soapbox in the public arena."

B238 Schott, Webster. "A Small Man Uncrushed by Brutal
Power," *Life*, LXI (September 16, 1966), 16.

"A vision of horrible pain and agonizing hope, *The Fixer*
shows us where fiction must go to repossess our
minds and feelings."

B239 Schroth, Raymond A. *America*, CXV (September 17,
1966), 284.

"Christian ... compassion for Malamud's creation may be
tempered by his conviction that suffering is not uniquely
Jewish. . . . Malamud has discussed the world's . . . and, I
believe, the author's ... rejection of Christ."

B240 "Shlemiel Triumphant," *Newsweek* LXIX (September
12, 1966), 108.

"By an imaginative master stroke, Malamud shifts the scene
from the external, public events to the internal, private
events of Yakov's ordeal . . . and the fixer resisted all attempts
to unman and dehumanize him."

B241 Snowden, Richard L. Chicago *Literary Review*, (May
1967), 12.

"A fine and moving book . . . which is comparable
to *The Brothers Karamazov* . . . but not that big a book."

B242 "Sons of Perdition," (London) *Times Literary
Supplement*, April 6, 1967, p. 286.

"The novel simultaneously invokes the solidarity of the Jews
and the solitariness of the individual Jew. . . . Whoever
becomes a Jew, becomes himself."

B243 Stella, Charles. "Malamud Adds to Literary Stature,"
Cleveland *Press*, September 9, 1966, p. 16.

"The indomnible (sic) will of Yakov Bok is a testament to men everywhere who will not be broken by the blows of tyranny, ignorant hate, and prejudice."

B244 Thorpe, Day. "Malamud's Powerful Novel about Justice," Washington *Star*, September 11, 1966, p. G-2.

"A powerful novel about injustice as it reacts upon a single man. . . . the true theme is an individual and injustice."

B245 *Time*, LXXXVIII (September 9, 1966), 106, 108.

"[*The Fixer*] misses by very little [being] a great novel. . . . [Malamud has written] a tragedy with a humanistic ending."

B246 Yardley, Rosemary. "In the Web of Life's Absurdities," Greensboro *Daily News*, September 11, 1966, p. D-3.

". . . The book is deceptively easy to read and annoyingly difficult to fathom."

A Malamud Reader

B247 Bail, Jay. "A War of the Proses," *The Patriot Ledger* (Quincy, Mass.), November 3, 1967, p. 30.

"Bernard Malamud, considered . . . to be around the top of the U.S. novelist heap, is essentially a short story writer. As can be seen in this collection of his works, when his novels are laid side by side with his short stories the results are disastrous. . . . From the sharp, relevant persecution of Fidelman in the short story, "The Last Mohican," we come to the dull, rather pointless persecution of Yakov in the recent Pulitzer Prize novel, *The Fixer*. . . . [The best novels] are intriguing mixtures of fantasy and realism packed together to give a fuller meaning to human misfortune, but they are still slightly flatter, less piercing than a good many of his short stories."

B248 Bannon, Barbara. *Publishers' Weekly*, CXCII (September 4, 1967), 50.

"A rich and satisfying anthology taken from the entire body of Malamud's work. . . . this should find adoption in many college classrooms."

B249 Dr. Rahv Evaluates Noted Author's Jewishness in *Malamud Reader*," Detroit *Jewish News*, November 10, 1967, p. 10.

This reviewer speaks of the value of Philip Rahv's introduction to the book as enriching "an enriching work." Among the "Jewish traits in Malamud's writings indicated by Professor Rahv is 'his feeling for human suffering on the one hand and for a life of value, order and dignity on the other'. . . . He notes that 'Malamud transcends all sectarian understanding of suffering, seeing it as the fate of the whole of mankind, which can only be mitigated when all men assume responsibility for each other.' "

B250 Dunn, Millard. "Needed: A Sense of Difference," *The Times*, (Roanoke, Virginia), December 17, 1967, p. C-18.

Dunn cites the belief of Professor Louis D. Rubin, Jr. that a "sense of difference is perhaps responsible for the success of the Jewish novelist. . . . Malamud is able to use what Professor Rubin calls 'the Experience of Difference' to show us how the human experience itself is one of difference, how. . . . it is through a resolution of this conflict of values that the novelist gives meaning and significance to his work, and through our application of his resolution to our own lives that the novel has meaning for us."

B251 Hulett, Frederick. "Vivid Characters," *Courier Post*, (Camden, New Jersey), November 25, 1967, p. 6.

"This is a writer who may join their [Faulkner's and Hemingway's] company. . . . The people and scenes are as 'ethnic' as Faulkner or Hemingway. . . . They have the quirks,

the accents, the sometimes abrasive and insistent humanism,
the grasp when required and the Christian charity when evoked,
of his born and chosen milieu. . . . The immersion, or
translation takes a little time. Malamud's inflection is so
perfect, his refinement of differences so microscopic, that a
reader who fails to be Jewish can for a moment be deflected.
As a reader may be in Faulkner, Hemingway, Steinbeck,
Emerson, Whitman, Thoreau. . . . Only a blunt sensibility will
fail to follow up."

B252 Hutchinson, J. D. "Jewish Heritage Enhances
Malamud's Work," *The Sunday Denver Post,*
December 3, 1967, p. 19.

Hutchinson agrees with Philip Rahv's opinion that
Malamud "distinguishes himself from the American school of
Jewish writers—Mailer, Roth, Bellow, etc.—in that he does
not retreat from or circumvent the Jewishness of his heritage
in his writing." He agrees with Rahv that the awareness of
Jewishness is "one of the principal sources of value in
[Malamud's] work as it affects both his conception
of experience in general and his conception of imaginative
writing in particular." Hutchinson cites the story "The Magic
Barrel" as an exemplar of the influence, calling it "one of
the most nearly classically perfect stories ever written."

B253 Lutz, Fred. "Compelling Sample of a Pivotal Artist,"
The Blade, (Toledo, Ohio), November 12, 1967,
Section J, p. 5.

Malamud is cited among other "new romantics who favor
mysticism (Salinger), fantasy (Dunleavy), hipsterism
(Mailer), passion (Baldwin), and suffering (Malamud). . . .
Malamud has . . . achieved the most solid body of work of
the lot, and possibly the most romantic. . . . Malamud is a
Jewish writer in the same sense that George Orwell was a
political writer or Upton Sinclair was a social-protest writer. He
concerns himself with this theme . . . in order to get at the
universality of suffering. . . . To accommodate his passionate,
suffering characters Malamud has developed a style both cool

and simple. The characters seem to speak for themselves without benefit of the medium of an author."

B254 Lynch, William S. "The First of Many," Providence *Journal*, November 2, 1967, "Rhode Islander" Section, p. 4.

Malamud creates "Job-like characters, ambivalent saints, someone has called them. . . . No author today is more compassionate than he, none more preoccupied with the sufferings of the human condition. Dostoevski inevitably comes to mind. . . . His stories have a universal quality which transcends anything as provincial as ethnic origin."

B255 McClintock, Jack. "More of Malamud," Tampa *Tribune*, November 5, 1967, "Florida Accent" Section, p. 3.

"This is a nice, plump collection of some of the best work of one of today's best writers. . . . Malamud, like all fine writers, rises above the critics [in this case, Philip Rahv, in his introduction to the volume] who would intellectualize all the juices out of his work with . . . tortured prose [analysis]. . . . He writes about life honestly, but with a modicum of optimism unusual in much modern fiction."

B256 Perley, Marc E. "The Best of Bernard Malamud Revisited," Louisville *Times*, November 9, 1967, p. 18.

"This intriguing compilation is of particular interest to literary lovers and students in that it reveals the virtuosity of one of America's most distinguished authors and illustrates some of his techniques. . . . This motif [an affirmation of life and of the dignity of the human personality] occurs and recurs both in the novels and short stories."

B257 R. Z. "Fiction is Actually Truth—Malamud," Hartford *Times*, November 1, 1967, p. 10.

"Fiction as [Malamud] tells it does bear a closer resemblance to truth than the work of nearly any other contemporary

writer. Malamud is producing fiction for the ages, as did
Tolstoy and similar giants."

B258 Yardley, Jonathan. Greensboro *Daily News*, October
29, 1967, p. B-3.

"With a totality of commitment perhaps unexceeded by any
other American writer of this era, Mr. Malamud pursues in
his work the truth about human existence; the world of the
imagination is the world in which we live. . . . If the truth is to
be found in his writing, it is in the stories he tells of human
triumph over adversity; of human beings, alone in a dismaying
world, who reach out to each other for comfort and
recognition. . . . Malamud's affirmation is profound precisely
because it does not come easily, to the reader or to him. Before
one can affirm human life one must suffer; meaningful
appreciation of its value and significance must be preceded by
an understanding of the costs we pay for our existence."